nuggets of faith

D1479051

Jack Hartman

Library of Congress Catalog Card Number 83-051359

"...of making of many books there is no end"
Ecclesiastes 12:12.

Printed by Custom Graphics, Tulsa, Oklahoma

"The Lord gave the word:
great was the company
of those that published it."
Psalm 68:11

First printing - 1/84 - 15,000 copies

Published by:

WORD ASSOCIATES

Introduction

The first six months of 1974 were dreary months in my life. I am a self-employed businessman and, due to a business collapse, I found myself in a position where my annual debt repayment obligations were considerably more than my annual income.

There didn't seem to be any way out. Everyone told me that I had no alternative except to file bankruptcy. I was in an extremely difficult financial position and I also was very close to a nervous breakdown. I can tell you from experience what a nervous breakdown is—it is a time in your life when you know that you can't take one more step emotionally no matter what the consequences might be.

I couldn't sleep at night. I worried all day, every day. All that I could think about was losing the home that our family had lived in for the past twelve years. I worried constantly about losing the business that I had worked so hard to build. I worried about what my family would think when we had to move out of our home and into a low rent apartment.

At that critical time in my life, a friend of mine told me that I didn't have to file bankruptcy. He told me that there *was* a way out of my problems. He explained to me why I needed to accept Jesus Christ as my Saviour. I made the great decision to invite Jesus into my life on July 20, 1974.

My friend then told me that the answer to every one of my problems was in the Bible. He told me that *every* word in the Bible was inspired by God Himself (II Timothy 3:16). He told me that the only way out of my problems was to "saturate" myself in God's Word—the Holy Bible.

This is exactly what I did. I studied the Scriptures day and night. I listened to hundreds of cassette tapes. I read hundreds of books. I really did "saturate" myself in the Scriptures.

From that very first day on July 20, 1974 I started to write what I called "Spiritual Meditations"—the spiritual truths that I had learned that day. I now have written over 20,000 (!) of these meditations and I continue to write them almost every day of life.

The "saturation" in God's Word worked beyond my fondest dreams. Every debt has been paid off as scheduled. Our business has prospered. We still live in the same home. I don't worry any more.

In addition to all of this, much more has happened in my life. In 1975 I started to meet with three other businessmen in the conference room of our office building. We studied the Bible and the Lord led me to teach these Bible studies.

Soon, our conference room was filled to overflowing. We had to move to a Holiday Inn. Then we moved to a larger room in a Sheraton Inn. Then we moved to a junior high school cafeteria. Finally, so many people were coming that we moved to a large high school auditorium.

Out of all of this has grown our church—Faith Christian Center. We now have approximately one thousand people in attendance each Sunday morning. I still teach the Tuesday night inter-denominational Bible study and approximately 30% of our audience comes from other churches.

A miracle has happened in my life and it happened because I surrendered my life to Jesus Christ and because I have faithfully studied and mediated day and night in God's Word ever since 1974. If all of this has happened to me, it *can* happen to you, too, because God doesn't play favorites. "...God is no respector of persons..." (Acts 10:34).

Over the years I have shared some of my "spiritual meditations" with several people.

Time and time again these people have told me how these short, simple, random thoughts have helped them.

This book is a summary of my best spiritual meditations on the subject of faith. I call them "Nuggets Of Faith." Read through these "nuggets." Use a pen. Underline, highlight or draw a rectangle around the ones that make sense to you. Meditate on them. Personalize them. Turn them over and over in your mind. Think how they apply to your life.

I pray that this unique, simple book of "nuggets of faith" will touch your life just as they have touched the lives of so many people who have attended our Bible studies.

1 How To Enter Into God's Kingdom

Every person who ever lived on this earth was born physically out of the womb of a human mother. Our most important decision in life is to be born a second time spiritually. Spiritual rebirth is required in order to enter into the kingdom of God. "...Except a man be born again, he *cannot* see the kingdom of God" (John 3:3).

God's great truths seem *foolish* to people who have not experienced a spiritual rebirth. "...the natural man receiveth *not* the things of the Spirit of God: for they are *foolishness* unto him: *neither* can he know them, because they are *spiritually* discerned" (I Corinthians 2:14).

When we are reborn spiritually, an entire new spiritual realm—the kingdom of God—is opened up to us. The veil that used to blind us spiritually is taken away. "...whenever anyone turns to the Lord from his sins, *then* the veil is taken away" (II Corinthians 3:16 *The Living Bible*).

(See Appendix of this book for an explanation of why and how we need to be born again spiritually.)

2 We Need To Focus On The Spiritual Realm—Not The Natural Realm

There are two separate realms in our lives—the natural realm (the realm of our senses) and the spiritual realm (the realm of our spirits). Millions of people focus on the realm that they can contact with their senses and ignore the spiritual realm.

This is wrong. Our Father's Word tells us that we should do just the opposite. "...look *not* at the things which are seen, but at the things which are *not seen*: for the things which are seen are *temporal*; but the things which are not seen are *eternal*" (II Corinthians 4:18).

It is a fact that everything in the tangible, natural realm actually came out of the spiritual realm. "...we know that the world and the stars—in fact, *all things*—were made at God's command; and that they were made from *nothing*!" (Hebrews 11:3 *The Living Bible*).

Through constant study and meditation in God's Word we will be able to transcend the natural realm which is only the "effect" and reach out into the spiritual realm which is the "cause." If we work diligently at this, our lives will be completely transformed.

3 It's Not Easy To Change The Habits Of A Lifetime

Many of us are not reborn spiritually until after we have spent several years living in a

10

non-Christian environment. During these years we built up many habits that are opposite from God's way of doing things. "...the carnal mind is *enmity* against God..." (Romans 8:7). The Greek word that is translated *enmity* means *enemy.* Carnal, worldly minds are opposed to God.

God has His way of doing things and He's not about to change. "For I am the Lord, I *change not...*" (Malachi 3:6). *We* are that ones who have to change the habits that we have developed. Our Father doesn't want our minds to be His enemy. He wants us on the same "wave length" that He is on.

4 God's Ways Are Not Mysterious

Have you ever heard someone say, "God works in mysterious ways His wonders to perform?" This sounds good, but it *doesn't* apply to God's children. When we are reborn spiritually, we enter into God's family and what used to be mysterious does not have to be mysterious any longer. "...it is given unto *you* to *know* the mysteries of the kingdom of heaven, but to *them* it is *not* given" (Matthew 13:11).

Our Father has given us a method of finding out His will for our lives. "Having *made known unto us* the mystery of his will..." (Ephesians 1:9). A will is a testament and our

11

Father has given us an Old Testament (before Jesus Christ) and a New Testament (after Jesus Christ).

Our Father wants us to fill our lives with knowledge of His will so that we will live fruitful lives that are pleasing to Him. "...desire that ye might be *filled with* the knowledge of his will in all wisdom and spiritual understanding; that ye might walk worthy of the Lord unto all pleasing, being fruitful in *every* good work, and *increasing* in the knowledge of God..." (Colossians 1:9-10).

5 We Must Work Hard To Learn God's Ways

When we're reborn spiritually, everything becomes new in the spiritual realm. "Therefore if any man be in Christ, he is a *new* creature: old things are *passed away;* behold, *all* things are become *new*" (II Corinthians 5:17).

Brand new horizons are available to us—to the exact degree that we are willing to pay the price of working hard at studying God's Word —the Holy Bible. If we want our Father to approve of us, we need to work diligently at studying His Word. "Study to shew thyself *approved* unto God, a workman that needeth *not* to be *ashamed,* rightly dividing the word of truth" (II Timothy 2:15).

If we'll pay the price of diligently studying our Father's Word, He will show us new ways that we could not see in our spiritual blindness. He will make light out of darkness and He will show us how to straighten out our lives. "And I will bring the blind by a way that they *knew not*; I will lead them in paths that they have not known: I will make *darkness light* before them, and *crooked things straight.* These things will I do unto them, and *not* forsake them" (Isaiah 42:16).

6 It Is Very Important For God's Children To Live By Faith

When we pay the price of diligently studying God's Word, one of the many spiritual dimensions that will open up to us is the dimension of faith. God's Word tells us how important it is for His children to live their lives based upon faith. "Now the just *shall live by faith*: but if any man shall *draw back*, my soul shall have *no pleasure* in him" (Hebrews 10:38).

Our Father is not at all pleased if we don't live by faith. We cannot please Him unless we live lives of faith. "...without faith *it is impossible* to please him; for he that cometh to God *must* believe that he *is*, and that he is a *rewarder* of them that diligently seek him" (Hebrews 11:6).

13

Why is it impossible to please God without faith? We can see this easily by comparing our heavenly Father with a human father here in the world. What earthly father would be pleased if he saw his children suffering unnecessarily simply because they didn't believe what he told them?

Our heavenly Father is no different. He has given us a Book which tells us exactly how He wants us to live our lives here on this earth. All that we need to do is to study this Book, find out the directions that He has given us and then follow these directions with faith that they *will* do what He said they would do. If He sees us suffering because we fail to follow His directions, of course He won't be pleased with us!

2 Where Does Faith Come From?

Faith comes from *hearing* the Word of God. "So then faith cometh by *hearing*, and hearing by *the word of God*" (Romans 10:17). Many people don't have much faith because they *hear* very little of God's Word. They go to churches where God's Word isn't preached very much. They seldom hear God's Word spoken by others and their ears seldom, if ever, hear God's Word spoken by their own lips. In my opinion, the greatest way to build up a

strong faith is for *our ears* to constantly hear
God's Word spoken by *our lips.*

8 We Must Be Very Careful What We Listen To

Jesus once told a multitude of people who
were listening to Him, "...*Take heed* what ye
hear: with what *measure* ye mete, it *shall* be
measured to you: and unto you that hear shall
more be given" (Mark 4:24).

What does this mean? It means that we
need to be careful what we listen to because
what we allow to come into our ears will be
multiplied. If we hear a lot of God's Word, this
will cause our faith to multiply. On the other
hand, if we allow our ears to constantly listen
to bad news, worries and fears, this will open
the door for a lot more of the same to come in.

9 The Difference Between Hope And Faith

Hope is in our *minds.* Faith is in our *hearts.*
We can see this in I Thessalonians 5:8 which
compares hope to a "helmet" and where faith is
called "the breastplate of faith." A helmet
obviously protects the mind and a breastplate
obviously protects the heart.

Hope has its function—it sets the goal for
faith. Hope wishes. Faith knows. Hope is
intangible. Faith is tangible. Faith gives sub-

stance to hope and brings it into being. "Now faith is the *substance* of things *hoped for*, the *evidence* of things *not seen*" (Hebrews 11:1).

10 Faith Reaches Into The Spiritual Realm

Faith is the line of communication between the natural world and the spiritual realm. Faith puts us into contact with our Father and enables us to reach out into the spiritual realm and bring our Father's promises *into* reality here in the natural world. These promises are manifested in exact proportion to the degree that we are able to release the spiritual power of faith.

11 Faith Requires Humility

Pride and faith do not go together! Pride says, "I am great. I can do it." Faith says, "I know that I can't do it, but I know that God *can* do it and I know that He *will* do it!" Faith and humility go together. Humility knows that we can't do it. Faith knows that our Father will do it.

We receive our Father's blessings to the exact degree that we realize our helplessness and, as a result, depend on Him. All sin is caused by a desire to be independent of God. Faith is the exact opposite of this. True faith depends totally upon God.

12 Faith Works By Love

Love is greater than faith. "There are three things that remain—faith, hope and love—and *the greatest of these is love*" (I Corinthians 13:13 *The Living Bible*). Our love for God is what enables us to trust Him. If we don't love our Father deeply and if we don't have some comprehension as to how much He loves us, it's not easy for us to trust Him.

This is why His Word tells us that faith works by love. "...faith which *worketh* by *love*" (Galatians 5:6). Some Christians have studied faith in great detail and followed all of the principles they have learned and still aren't getting results. This often is caused by lack of love.

Our Father *commands* us to love one another (I John 3:23-24). Since faith works as a result of love it is easy to see how faith can be blocked by failing to follow our Father's commandment to love.

13 Faith Requires Us To Forgive Ourselves And Others

God's Word tells us that we won't be able to trust Him for anything until we first of all are able to *forgive ourselves*. "Beloved, *if* our heart *condemn us not, then* have we confidence *toward God*..." (I John 3:21). A guilty con-

17

science often blocks faith from working.

We can get rid of this. Our Father wants to forgive us and cleanse us of all sins. We simply have to go to Him and openly confess the error of our ways. "*If* we *confess* our sins, he *is* faithful and just to *forgive* us our sins, and to *cleanse* us from *all* unrighteousness" (I John 1:9). Our Father will forgive our sins. He will also *forget* them. "And their sins and iniquities will I *remember no more*" (Hebrews 10:17).

If our Father is willing to forgive our sins, then we must be willing to do the same—with ourselves and with others. If we don't, this unforgiveness will stop our faith from working.

14 We Must Be Willing To Pay A Price In Order To Build Strong Faith

Never in the history of Christianity have we seen the amount of material on faith that is available to us today. Hundreds of books and thousands of cassette tapes on the subject of faith are available to us. This is good. However, in the midst of this abundance of material on faith, there have been many instances of Christians who have become extremely frustrated when this "faith teaching" did not produce results in their lives.

In many cases, this is caused by a failure to build their faith properly. Faith is progressive in nature. It must be built one step at a time.

Many Christians become discouraged from trying to move spiritual "mountains" when their faith isn't strong enough to move these mountains. Instead of becoming discouraged and saying "This faith stuff doesn't work," we must be willing to pay the price of building our faith solidly, day after day, week after week, and month after month. It doesn't happen over night.

15 Faith Must Be Built Upon A Solid Foundation

For several years before I gave my life to Jesus Christ, I traveled in the United States and Canada giving speeches on positive thinking. These speeches were well received. I had carefully studied over a hundred "self help" books, I was well versed in their teachings and I was able to communicate these teachings to the audiences I spoke to.

However, when my whole world collapsed in 1974, I found that all of my theories on positive thinking *didn't* hold up under extreme pressure. These theories didn't have a solid foundation that would hold up under pressure. Since then, I have put a solid foundation under these theories and that solid foundation is the Word of God—the Holy Bible.

The principles of positive thinking that I taught *were* mostly correct. I *still* use most of these principles today, but *now* they are based on the awesome power of God's Word—the power that created the world that we live in and all of the other planets in this universe. "...the worlds were framed *by the word of God*..." (Hebrews 11:3). "*By the word of the Lord* were the heavens made..." (Psalm 33:6).

16 There Is Only One Tangible Connection Between The Natural Realm And The Spiritual Realm

The natural realm and the spiritual realm have only *one* common denominator. What is the *one* and *only thing* that we can see and touch and hear in the natural realm that *also* exists in the spiritual realm??? The answer is the Word of God. This clearly indicates why it is so important for us to study and meditate constantly in God's Word. It is in a class by itself. Nothing else is even remotely like it.

17 God's Word Will Reach Deep Down Inside Of Us

God's Word is *so* unique and powerful that it can reach deep down inside of us, *penetrating* to the dividing line between soul and the spirit, showing us *exactly* what we are like deep down inside ourselves. "For the word of God is quick, and powerful, and sharper than any two-edged sword, *piercing even to the dividing asunder of soul and spirit,* and of the joints and marrow, and is *a discerner of the thoughts and intents of the heart"* (Hebrews 4:12).

18 We Can Depend Completely On God's Word

Our Father has given us a Book that is filled with promises that we *can* rely on—no matter what happens in our lives. When everything is going wrong, it's very easy to come unglued and fall apart. This is exactly when we need to turn to God's Word *just* as we would turn to God Himself if He came to us in this time of great need.

Christianity is based upon believing the promises of God's Word about spending eternity in heaven because of the price that Jesus Christ paid for us. *If* we are able to trust completely in what God's Word says about *after we die,* then *why* shouldn't we trust its promises *just as much* during the remainder of our lives on earth???

God's Word will *never* fail. Any failure in our lives is caused by *our* lack of knowledge and/or faith in God's Word. The Holy Bible is not just another book containing words of man. This Book contains the words of God Himself and they *will* work to the exact degree that we *believe* that they will. "...when ye received the

21

word of God which ye heard of us, ye received it *not* as the word of man, but as it *is* in truth, the word of God which effectually *worketh* also in you that *believe*" (I Thessalonians 2:13).

19 Shouldn't We Be Able To Trust God More Than We Trust A Good Friend?

When a trusted friend tells us something, most of us don't have any hesitation whatever in acting upon what that trusted friend has told us. *Why* then, should we have any hesitation about stepping out in faith on the promises that our Creator has made to us? God and His Word are one and the same. We *can* put all of our weight on the promises of God's Word and they will hold us up.

Our Father's Word *is* completely reliable. "He has given us both His promise and His oath, two things we can completely *count* on, for it is *impossible* for God to tell a lie..." (Hebrews 6:18 *The Living Bible*). If we don't have faith in God's Word, this lack of faith actually says that God is a liar. "...he that believeth *not* God hath *made him a liar*..." (I John 5:10).

20 God's Promises Enable Us To Partake Of His Divine Nature

Our Father has given us a Book full of precious promises that, if followed, will enable us to be *partakers of His divine nature* and, as a result, we will be able to *escape* the corruption that surrounds us in this world. "Whereby are given unto us exceeding great and precious promises: that *by these* ye might be *partakers of the divine nature*, having *escaped* the corruption that is in the world through lust" (II Peter 1:4).

21 I Can't Get Enough Of God's Word!

In the world, we usually get tired of things if we partake of them constantly. God's Word is just the opposite. The same God who created us has given us every answer that any of us will ever need. What an awesome truth this is! I can't get enough of God's Word. I collect verses of Scripture. I have them around me at all times—on my lamp, on my telephone, on my wall, on cards and in notebooks. I am awash in a sea of Scripture.

The Bible is like a gigantic jigsaw puzzle. Our Father has given us *every* answer that we'll ever need, *but* these answers are cut up into little pieces and scattered throughout His Book. Our job is to find the pieces that go together and then to fit them together one piece at a time. "For precept must be upon precept, precept upon precept; line upon line, line upon line; here a little, and there a little..." (Isaiah 28:10).

22 We Should Not Eat Spiritual "Junk Food!"

Many of us are much more conscious of the food that goes into our bodies than we are about the spiritual food which is fed into our spirits. Many Christians who wouldn't dream of eating a lot of the "junk food" that is so prevalent today allow a great deal of spiritual "junk food" into their spirits.

Instead of allowing a lot of carnal, worldly books, movies and television to be fed into our spirits, we should feed our spirits constantly with the pure, wholesome Word of God. It is much *more* important to feed our spirits properly each day than it is to feed our bodies. "...I have esteemed and treasured up the words of His mouth *more than* my necessary food" (Job 23:12 *The Amplified Bible*).

23 Lack Of Knowledge Causes Severe Problems

We might be able to get by for many years without studying God's Word, but sooner or later this lack of knowledge will destroy us. "*My people* are *destroyed* for lack of knowledge: because thou hast *rejected* knowledge, I will also *reject* thee..." (Hosea 4:6).

This *doesn't* say that *sinners* will be destroyed for lack of knowledge. Our Father's Word says "*My people* are destroyed for lack of knowledge..." As I write these words, I soon will start my ninth year of teaching the Bible. The most difficult thing for me to understand is *why* so many Christians absolutely *refuse* to pay the price of studying the Bible on a definite, continuing basis.

24 Stick To It!

Knowledge comes from repetition. We need to keep studying and meditating in God's Word—over and over and over—before it really settles into our spirits and becomes part of us. Many Christians start on a Bible study program, but very few people seem to have the desire, determination, dedication and discipline to stick to it month after month and year after year.

Yet, this is what we must do if we expect our Father to reward us. "...he is a rewarder of them that *diligently* seek him" (Hebrews 11:6). We need to study God's Word constantly. "...Man shall not live by bread alone, but by *every* word that proceedeth out of the mouth of God" (Matthew 4:4).

Jesus told us how to become His disciples. He told us exactly what we should do to become free from whatever problems we're faced with. He said that we need to get into His Word and *stay* there. If we do this, we will *know* the truth that we need to know and this truth will make us *free*. "...If ye *continue* in my word, *then* are ye my *disciples* indeed; and ye shall *know* the truth, and the truth shall make you *free*" (John 8:31-32).

25 The Best Deal I Ever Made

Several years ago I traded gigantic worries and fears for constant study and meditation in God's Word. This is the best deal that I have ever made in my life! I'll gladly trade the many hours that I spend in God's Word for the fears, worries and uncertainties that used to consume me.

If we'll spend large amounts of time in the presence of the Master, we'll obtain more and more of His calmness and strength. As we grow more and more in the Lord, the problems in life that used to defeat us will now be taken in stride and we won't be disturbed in the least by them.

26 Define the Problem

I believe that a problem that is well defined is already half way towards a solution. I believe that the first thing that a Christian should do in preparing to start a Bible study is to define his or her primary problems.

What's bugging you? Is it fear?...worry?...
sickness?...financial problems?...marriage problems?...problems with your children?...unhap-
piness?...anger?...bitterness?...envy?...lack of peace?
...lack of fulfillment?...or something else?

If we are grappling with problems in our
lives, doesn't it make sense for our Bible study
to be *specifically aimed* at solving *these* problems? Yet, I see many Christians with signifi-
cant problems who spend their Bible study
time studying something that doesn't have any
thing to do with helping them to find a
solution to these problems. Amazing...but true!

27 We Must Not Think That We Know More Than We Do

Sometimes Christians think that they know
a lot more about God's Word than they do.
"...Knowledge *puffeth up*..." (I Corinthians 8:1).
Beware of this trap. It's easy to believe that
our faith is strong when all is well, but the
only way to find out is to see how we react
when the bottom falls out. Don't ever let up.
It's impossible to know too much about the
instructions that our Father has given us.

28 Is God Really First?

In His great Sermon on the Mount Jesus said, "...seek ye *first* the kingdom of God, and his righteousness; and *all* these things *shall* be added unto you" (Matthew 6:33). Whatever our needs are, those needs *will* be met if we *really do* seek God first ahead of all else.

In truth, many of us who think that we keep God first, actually allow other things to get between God and ourselves. Of course church events are important. Of course family events are important. It is so easy to get caught up in these and similar areas of our lives and then to think "I just don't have time to study the Bible."

This is wrong! Whenever *anything*, no matter how important it might seem, comes ahead of our quiet time with the Lord, our priorities are wrong. What would you do if Jesus came to your house today? Wouldn't you put everything aside in order to spend time with Him??

Jesus comes to your house every day of your life! He comes through the Word of God. Jesus and the Word of God are *one and the same* (John 1:1 and 1:14). *Are you* setting aside time every day—ahead of everything else—to learn from the Master??

29 Of Course We Can Get Up One Hour Earlier!

Sometimes Christians tell me how hard it is to get up one hour earlier each morning to study God's Word. This simply is not true. In the section of the United States where I live, we adjust our clocks twice each year. We move them forward one hour in the spring and backward one hour in the fall. Everyone seems to adjust to this without any problems.

If we can adjust our sleeping habits twice each year because government regulations tell us to, why can't we voluntarily make a similar adjustment in order to study the instructions that our Father has given us?

30 Worry Is Scriptural Meditation In Reverse

Joshua 1:8, Psalms 1:1-3 and other verses of Scripture tell us about the great importance of meditating constantly in God's Word. I believe that meditation means to fix our attention on a particular verse (or verses) of Scripture and to turn this scripture over and over in our minds—looking at it from every angle and personalizing it to see how these instuctions from our Father apply to our own situation.

Have you ever thought that this is *exactly* what we do if we worry? Worriers focus in on a particular problem that they're afraid will come into their lives. They look at it from every angle, worrying about how this will affect their lives.

Worriers, it's time to switch your meditation—from meditating on problems to meditating on the solutions that our Father has given us!

31 Our Minds Need To Be Made "Brand New"

When we are reborn spiritually, God gives us a brand new spirit, but we still have the same mind. God's Word was *not* conceived by a carnal, worldly mind and it *cannot* be understood by a carnal, worldly mind! God's Word only can be understood to the degree that we are willing to *renew* our minds—to *make them new*—through continual study and meditation in God's Word.

Our Father wants us to *change* our thinking from the way that the world thinks to the way that He thinks. To the degree that we do this, we'll see exactly how He wants us to live our lives and our lives will be *transformed*. "And be *not* conformed to this world: but be ye *transformed* by the *renewing* of your mind, that ye may *prove* what is that good, and acceptable, and perfect, will of God" (Romans 12:2).

As we grow older, our physical bodies decay. Our Father wants us to counteract this through a spiritual "fountain of youth"—by renewing the inner man—the spiritual being inside of us—*every day.* "...Though our *outer* man is (progressively) *decaying* and *wasting away,* yet our *inner self* is being (progressively) renewed day after day" (II Corinthians 4:16 *The Amplified Bible).*

32 Many Christians Never Even Get Into "Spiritual Kindergarten"

After we're born again spiritually, we need to "clean up" our minds in order to get rid of the pride, selfishness, worries, fears and all of the incorrect beliefs that have developed over the years. Unfortunately, many Christians never grow past the point of spiritual infancy. Our Father wants us to pay the price to grow out of spiritual infancy into spiritual childhood, spiritual adolescence and spiritual maturity. Only by doing this will we be able to escape spiritual death and, as a result, to experience God's great peace for our lives. "For to be *carnally* minded is death; but to be *spiritually* minded is *life* and *peace*" (Romans 8:6).

31

33 We Need To Strengthen Our Minds

Our minds need to be strengthened constantly. God's Word says, "...*gird up the loins* of your mind..." (I Peter 1:13). The Greek word that is translated *gird* means that we should *strengthen* our minds. The word *loins* means the *reproductive center* of our minds.

We need to strengthen our minds—to brace them up—through constant study and meditation in God's Word. This study and meditation should be *so* effective that it will penetrate into the very *center* of our minds, reproducing itself in the form of additional spiritual strength.

34 We Must Be Patient In Our Study Of God's Word

It's not easy for most of us to make the breakthrough from the way that we have done things for many years to God's way of doing things. This doesn't happen overnight. This requires hundreds and hundreds of hours of study and meditation in God's Word.

When I first started this study and meditation in God's Word, I was in a seemingly hopeless situation financially and my life was full of worry and fear. During my first few months of study and meditation, my situation got *worse* and I really *wasn't* getting much out of my Bible study. In fact, I often found it boring and difficult to comprehend.

In spite of this, I was patient. Even though I didn't see any immediate results, I knew deep down inside of myself that I was on the right track. I didn't stop. I kept going. Finally, the first breakthrough came followed by more and more and more fresh, vital revelations.

I'm *so* thankful that I stuck with it even though my early efforts didn't seem to be producing any results. I urge you to do the same!

35 Our Spirits Must Take Control

When our Father created us, He made us with three separate parts—spirit, soul and body. Our spirits operate in the spiritual realm, our souls operated in the intellectual realm and our bodies operate in the physical realm. The reason for most of the frustration in the world is that so many people are trying to solve problems in the intellectual and physical realms that can *only* be solved in the spiritual realm.

God's Word is not addressed to our intellects. It is addressed to our spirits. The more we study and meditate in God's Word, the more our intellects will be made new and the more they will *align themselves* with our recreated spirits.

The more that this process takes place, the more our spirits will dominate our souls and our bodies. Then we'll be living our lives the way our Father wants us to live them—with our spirits controlling our souls and our bodies in last place where they belong.

36 Spirit First— Then Soul—Then Body

Some Christians say "body, soul and spirit" instead of "spirit, soul and body." I believe that the way that we arrange these three words is a subconscious indication of the degree of emphasis that we place upon each of them.

37 Jesus Christ Spent A Great Deal Of "Quiet Time" With His Father

Many Christians are so busy that they can't seem to find time to be alone with God. Isn't it interesting that Jesus Christ, the most success-ful man who ever lived on this earth, never had this problem? The Scriptures tell us on several occasions that Jesus went off to spend "quiet time" alone with His Father.

If Jesus was able to do this, we can do this too. It is very important for us to give top priority to our quiet time with the Lord. Nothing should take precedence over this time.

Although it may not seem like it, this is the most important time that any of us will spend during our lives here on this earth. This is the time that our Father will use to prepare us for the work that He has for us.

During this time with the Lord we need to meditate, to study, to pray and to worship the Lord. These precious hours will strengthen, renew and refresh us. Every bit of strength, peace, joy and wisdom that I have comes from this quiet time with the Lord. I wouldn't miss it for anything.

38 A Precious Room

I have spent precious hours with the Lord behind the wheel of my car, while I was exercising and in hotel rooms all over America and Canada, but when I'm home I have one room where I have spent several thousand hours alone with the Lord.

This room is a small downstairs room in our home. Numerous pictures of Jesus and verses of Scripture are on the wall. The room is filled with Bibles, Bible commentaries, Bible dictionaries, Bible handbooks, Christian books and Christian cassette tapes.

Most weeks I spend between fifteen and twenty hours alone with the Lord in this room. He and I have spent thousands of hours together here over the years and it is the most precious place in my life. Once when someone asked me the favorite vacation place that I had ever been to, I replied that it is the little room downstairs in our home.

39 We Believe With Our Hearts— Not Our Minds

Our Father gave us a mind to think with and a heart to believe with. Many people make the mistake of trying to believe with their minds. This can't be done. "For *with the heart* man believeth..." (Romans 10:10).

The key to every aspect of our lives is what we really believe—deep down inside of our hearts. We should study and meditate so much in God's Word that it passes from our minds down into our hearts and actually "abides" in us. Jesus said, "If ye *abide* in me, and my words *abide* in you, ye shall ask *what ye will*, and it *shall* be done unto you" (John 15:7).

When we abide in Christ, this means that everything in our lives is centered around Him. When this is added to His Word abiding inside of us, He says that our prayers *will* be answered. This is also the way to overcome our enemy Satan. "...the word of God *abideth* in you, and ye have *overcome* the wicked one" (I John 2:14).

40 The Greatest Security In This World Is A Heart That Is Filled With God's Word

In these difficult times, people are increasingly interested in security. Too many people are looking for security outside of themselves. This is wrong. The greatest security that any of us can have is a heart that is filled to overflowing with God's Word. Our Father wants His Word to establish permanent residence in our hearts. He wants us to become one with His Word and His Word to become one with us.

We need to work diligently at filling our hearts with God's Word because *every* issue in our lives is determined by *what we believe in our hearts.* "*Keep* thy heart with *all diligence;* for *out of it* are *the issues of life*" (Proverbs 4:23). We become what we are in our hearts. "For as he thinketh in his *heart,* so is he..." (Proverbs 23:7).

In the natural realm, our hearts must be strong physically for our bodies to function well. In the spiritual realm, it is even more important for our hearts to be strong spiritually. We must pay the price of getting God's Word deep down in our hearts so that it will take root and grow. If we don't do this, our faith won't be strong enough when we really need it. "And have *no root* in themselves, and *so endure but for a time...*" (Mark 4:17).

41 The Established Heart Cannot Be Moved

A doubting heart is a heart that is ruled by our senses and emotions—a heart that reacts primarily to what we see, what we hear and/or how we feel. An established heart is a heart which *cannot* be moved. It is *full* of God's Word and it does *not* react to the bad news of the world. Fear *cannot* get in. *"Surely* he shall *not* be moved *for ever:* the righteous shall be *in everlasting* remembrance. He shall *not be afraid* of evil tidings: his heart is *fixed*, trusting in the Lord. His heart is *established*, he shall *not be afraid..."* (Psalm 112:6-8).

42 How Have You Programmed Your "Computer?"

External problems must *not* be allowed to get down into our hearts. *How* can we prevent this? This is done by having *so much* of God's Word in our hearts that these problems are *unable* to get in.

Our minds are like computers and our hearts are where our "computers" store their data. When a negative thought tries to come into our minds, these "computers" immediately search the data that is stored up in the heart. If the appropriate promise from God's Word is found during this search, it will pop up and *reject* the negative thought. *"Casting down*

38

imaginations, and *every* high thing that exalt-eth itself *against* the knowledge of God, and bringing into captivity *every thought* to the obedience of Christ..." (II Corinthians 10:5).

43 Jesus Wants Us To "Cast" All Of Our "Cares" Upon Him

I often hear Christians say, "I'd like to give all of my problems to the Lord, but I just can't let go of them." God's Word tells us *exactly* how to do this. "... be *clothed with humility:* for God *resisteth* the *proud*, and giveth *grace* to the *humble*. *Humble* yourselves therefore under the mighty hand of God, that he may *exalt you* in due time: *casting all your care* upon him; for he careth for you" (I Peter 5:5-7).

What does this mean? First of all, we are told that we should be "clothed with humility," *completely covered* by humility. *Why* is it so important for us to be humble? Because our Father will actually be forced to *resist* us if we are proud! On the other hand, if we are humble, He will give us grace—blessings that we *don't* deserve.

God *will* lift us up (in due time) *if* we continually humble ourselves before Him. When we are proud, we have difficulty casting our cares on the Lord because we think that we have to carry them *ourselves!* When we insist on trying to solve all of our own problems, *this is pride.* Whether we consciously realize it or not, we're actually saying to God, *"I* can take care of this. I *don't* need you." God *resists* this prideful attitude.

Our Father wants us to realize how inadequate our human abilities are and how great and awesome He is. When we truly comprehend this, we *won't* hesitate to trust Him with all of our problems. We must realize how foolish it is to try to solve every problem with our strength.

44 Let God Be God

Too many of us get into trouble trying to carry burdens that God is meant to carry. We need to stop trying to be God and let Him be God! We need to stop trying to do His job and start doing our job. Our job is to constantly build our faith so that it will be strong enough to trust Him to carry the burdens that we are unable to carry.

As we have just seen in I Peter 5:7, Jesus wants us to *cast* all of our cares upon Him. The Greek word that is translated *cast* means to *throw.* Think of a fisherman casting. He "throws" his line out into the water. Jesus wants us to "throw" our worries and cares to Him. He *doesn't* want us hanging onto them. He wants us to *let go completely* because we trust completely in Him.

45 Take Off That Weight

In the natural world, millions of people are trying to lose weight. We *also* need to lose weight in the spiritual realm. "...let us *lay aside every weight,* and the sin which doth so easily beset us, and let us run with *patience* the race that is set before us, *looking unto Jesus* the author and finisher of our faith..." (Hebrews 12:1-2).

A lot of us are carrying around a lot of spiritual weight that we shouldn't be carrying. It is bad for our spiritual health. We need to get rid of it. We *can* lose this spiritual weight simply by giving this load to Jesus.

We've got to keep ourselves in good spiritual condition. Our Father doesn't want us carrying these heavy spiritual loads. He wants us to do our spiritual exercises every day so that we will stay in good spiritual condition and keep that spiritual weight off.

46 Jesus Wants Us To Use His Strength

Christians have the awesome strength of Jesus Christ available to them. How *foolish* it is to struggle and strain trying to do everything with our human strength when we have the strength of Jesus Christ available to us.

41

However, this is exactly what many Christians do.

Jesus wants us to use His strength, but he *doesn't* force it on us. He'll give us His strength to the exact degree that we *realize* our own weakness and, as a result, *turn* to Him, *trusting* in His strength. "And he said unto me, My grace *is* sufficient for thee: for *my strength* is made *perfect* in *weakness*. Most gladly therefore will I rather *glory in my infirmities*, in reproaches, in necessities, in persecutions, in distresses for Christ's sake: for *when I am weak, then am I* strong" (II Corinthians 12:9-10).

The world hates to admit weakness. In the world, it is "macho" to be strong and self-sufficient. This is exactly the *opposite* of the teaching of God. His Word says, "He giveth power to *the faint;* and to them that have *no might* he increaseth strength" (Isaiah 40:29).

47 The Weak Should Say That They Are Strong

Christians should never allow their mouths to say that they are weak or that they don't have enough strength. If we feel weak, God's Word tells us to open our mouths and to acknowledge *His* strength. "...let the *weak* say, I am *strong*" (Joel 3:10).

We should never acknowledge a feeling of weakness. We need to say what God's Word says, not how we feel. God's Word says, "I *can* do *all* things *through Christ* which *strengtheneth* me" (Philippians 4:13).

The Lord wants us to use *His* strength, *not* ours. "...be strong *in the Lord*, and in the power of *his might*" (Ephesians 6:10). We *won't* win the difficult battles of life with *our* strength. "...a mighty man is *not* delivered by much strength" (Psalm 33:16). We need to constantly seek the Lord's strength. "Seek the Lord and *his strength...*" (Psalm 105.4).

The closer we draw to God, the stronger we will become and the more we will be able to accomplish through His strength. "...the people that do *know* their God shall *be strong*, and do exploits" (Daniel 11:32). We should find our strength in the joy of an all-conquering, Almighty, totally victorious Jesus Christ. "...the *joy* of the Lord is *your strength*" (Nehemiah 8:10).

48 Great Human Abilities Are Not Sufficient

Although it may not seem that way, one of the worst things that can happen to many people is to have great human abilities—either physically or intellectually. When we have great abilities, it is very easy to depend on them even though God's Word says, "...the race is *not* to the swift, *nor* the battle to the strong..." (Ecclesiastes 9:11).

This dependence on self is especially noticeable with many young people. The youthful strength and vibrancy that flows through them often makes them feel as though they can do anything. God's Word warns against trusting in this youthful strength and tells us to place our trust in Him. *"Even the youths* shall faint and be weary, and *the young men shall utterly fall:* but they that *wait upon the Lord* shall renew *their strength;* they shall mount up with wings as *eagles;* they shall run, and *not* be weary; and they shall walk, and *not* faint." (Isaiah 40:30-31).

49 How To Receive More Of Jesus

I have heard a Christian song that is titled "I Want More Of Jesus." This is a nice title, but I believe that it is scripturally inaccurate. God's Word tells us that we *already* have *all* that there is to have. "And of his *fulness* have *all* we received..." (John 1:16).

Jesus has already given us *everything*. He gave us His very life. If we want to experience more of the fullness of Jesus Christ which has already been given to us, we *will* receive this in exact proportion to the degree that we give Him *more of ourselves!* This is God's law—

whatever we want to receive, we *first* of all need to *give*.

50 We Can Only Do Two Things For Jesus

It is natural for grateful Christians to want to do things for Jesus. However, we can only do two things for Jesus—*surrender* every area of our lives to Him and *trust* completely in Him. Jesus doesn't need our help. He needs our obedience and our faith.

Our Lord isn't looking for extraordinary people. Instead, He is looking for ordinary people who are completely willing to obey Him and trust Him in every area of their lives. We will always find Jesus Christ in *one* place— when we come to the *end* of ourselves. This is when Jesus will take over...to the exact degree that we yield to Him and trust in Him.

51 We Receive God's God's Holy Spirit By Faith

In the world, sinful men give gifts to their children. Our Father will give us the greatest gift that we can ever receive if we'll just *ask* Him and then *receive* this gift by *faith* in His Word. "If ye then, being evil, know how to give good gifts unto your children: *how much more* shall your heavenly Father *give the Holy Spirit to them that ask him?*" (Luke 11:13).

52 The Holy Trinity Lives Inside Of Us

It is difficult to comprehend with our limited human reasoning, but we have the entire Holy Trinity—the Father, the Son and the Holy Spirit living inside of us.

(1) God Himself lives inside of us. "One God and Father of all, who is above all, and through all, and *in you all*" (Ephesians 4:6).

(2) Jesus Christ lives inside of us. "...Christ liveth *in me...*" (Colossians 1:27).

(3) Because we are sons of God, our Father has sent His Holy Spirit to live inside of our hearts. "And because ye are sons, God hath sent forth the Spirit of His Son *into your hearts...*" (Galatians 4:6).

Can there *ever* be *any* problems in *any* of our lives that cannot be handled with *all of this power* living inside of us???

53 We Need To Trust Completely in God's Holy Spirit

Jesus Christ said, "I can *of mine own self do nothing...*" (John 5:30). Jesus told us how all of the great work was done in His life when He said, "...the Father that dwelleth in me, *he doeth the works*" (John 14:10).

The *same* Holy Spirit who raised Jesus Christ from the dead lives inside of us. "...the

Spirit of him that raised up Jesus from the dead *dwell in you...*" (Romans 8:11). What awesome power we have living inside of us!! God's Holy Spirit is able to do everything that we think He can, everything that we ask Him to do and *much, much more.* "Now glory be to God who by His mighty power at work within us is able to do *far more* than we would ever dare to ask or even dream of—*infinitely beyond* our highest prayers, desires, thoughts or hopes" (Ephesians 3:20 *The Living Bible).*

There is only *one* limit to the power of God's Holy Spirit who lives inside of us. That is whatever limit *we* place on Him due to *our* lack of faith in what He can and *will* do through us. We have the same power living inside of us who created heaven and earth. *Nothing* is too hard for Him. "Ah Lord God! behold, thou hast made the heaven and the earth by thy great power and stretched out arm, and *there is nothing too hard for thee...*" Jeremiah 32:17).

54 God's Holy Spirit Should Be The Center Of Our Lives

Every minute of every hour of every day of our lives should be built around God's Holy Spirit living inside of us. He should be the "hub" around which every area of lives revolves. The awareness of His awesome power should permeate deep into every fiber of our being. No matter what we come up against in this world, He *can* handle it. "Ye *are* of God, little children, and *have* overcome them: because *greater* is *he that is in you,* than *he that is in the world*" (I John 4:4).

We must be careful that we don't "mentally assent" to the great power of God's Holy Spirit living inside of us and *then* try to solve everything with our *own* ability. It is sad to see Christians who say that God's Holy Spirit lives inside of them forgetting all about Him as they struggle and strain trying to solve difficult problems with their limited human abilities.

55 Do You Realize What God's Holy Spirit Will Do For You?

I like the Amplified Bible version of Jesus' description of the Holy Spirit. "And I will ask the Father, and He will give you another *Comforter (Counselor, Helper, Intercessor, Advocate, Strengthener* and *Standby)* that He may remain with you *forever*" (John 14:16 *The Amplified Bible).*

How awesome this is! God sends His Holy Spirit to live inside of us *forever.* He is there to *comfort* us, to *help* us, to *intercede* for us, to *counsel* and *advise* us, to *strengthen* us and to *stand by* us. It is beyond human ability to describe the wonder of having such a friend living inside of us every minute of every hour of every day of our lives. He is our *closest* friend. "...there *is* a friend that sticketh *closer than a brother*" (Proverbs 18:24).

56 We Are Never Alone— The Lord Is Always With Us

How can a Christian *ever* be *lonely* if God's Holy Spirit lives inside of us and goes everywhere that we go? "...God hath said, I will *dwell in them,* and *walk in them;* and I *will* be their God, and they *shall* be my people" (II Corinthians 6:16).

There is absolutely nothing to be afraid of. God is with us *always.* "Fear thou *not,* for *I am with thee:* be *not* dismayed; for I *am* thy God: I *will* strengthen thee; yea, I *will* help thee; yea, I *will* uphold thee with the right hand of my righteousness" (Isaiah 41:10).

Our Lord Jesus Christ is with us always. He won't ever leave us or forsake us. "...for he hath said, *I will never leave thee, nor forsake thee.* So that we may boldly say, The Lord *is* my helper, and *I will not fear* what man shall do unto me" (Hebrews 13:5-6).

When we're going through the most difficult times of our lives, the Lord *is* with us and He *will* protect us if we put our trust in Him and show this trust by our words and by our actions in times of great adversity. "When thou passeth through the waters, I *will* be with thee; and through the rivers, they shall *not* overflow thee: when thou walkest through the fire, thou shalt *not* be burned; *neither* shall the flame kindle upon thee" (Isaiah 43:2).

57 God Knows Exactly What He Wants To Do In Our Lives

God lives inside of us and He knows exactly what He wants to do through us. "For *it is God which worketh in you* both *to will and to do* of *his* good pleasure" (Philippians 2:13). The ability of God lives inside of us. Our main function on this earth is to *get ourselves out of the way* and let God's great ability come out through us doing whatever *He wants to do* with our lives.

58 We Are Able To Block The Immense Power Of God's Holy Spirit

As mighty as God's Holy Spirit is and as weak as we are, we are still able to block this immense power that is inside of us. *How* do we block the Holy Spirit? We block Him in many ways—through dependency on self, pride, selfishness, distrust, worry, fear, anger, resentment, unforgiveness, hatred and similar self-centered, negative actions.

God's Holy Spirit speaks to us constantly. Like a radio station, we can hear His still, small voice clearly only if we are able to "tune in" to the exact "wave length" that He is on. We tune in to Him to the exact degree that we have yielded to Him to guide us in our study in God's Word. "...when he, the Spirit of truth is come, *he will guide you into all truth...*" (John 16:13).

59 How Do We Become Filled With God's Holy Spirit?

God's perfect will for our lives here on this earth is for every day of our lives to be filled with His Holy Spirit. *How* do our lives become filled with God's Holy Spirit? They become filled the same way that anything else is filled—to the exact degree that it is *empty*.

God's Holy Spirit will fill us to the degree that we *empty ourselves* of self-trust, self-reliance and self-importance. As we empty ourselves of "self" and yield more and more to God's Holy Spirit within us, surrendering to Him and trusting Him, He will fill us more and more. "...be *filled with* the Spirit; *speaking to yourselves* in *psalms* and *hymns* and *spiritual songs, singing* and *making melody in your heart to the Lord...*" (Ephesians 5:18,19).

The Spirit-filled life is a great and awesome life—a life that is totally different from any-

51

thing that we can ever experience in the worldly realm. When we *know* that God's Holy Spirit is in charge we will constantly open our mouths to *speak* God's Word and *praise* Him. Our mouths and our hearts will constantly be *filled* with spiritual *songs* and *melodies.*

60 Are Your Problems Bigger Than Your Solutions?

I have counseled with hundreds of Christians when they were in the midst of very difficult problems. In almost every case, I have found that they have placed *much more* emphasis on the *problems* in their lives than they did on the *solutions* to these problems in God's Word.

Time and time again these people have given me a detailed, emotional description of their problems. I often ask them what they think the solution is. Not one in one hundred of these troubled people will come back with specific promises from God's Word.

Christians who continually study and meditate in God's Word and yield constantly to God's Holy Spirit within them *will be able to see beyond the problem!* Instead of focusing constantly on the problem and worrying about the problem, they will keep their minds on God and trust completely in Him. "Thou wilt keep him in *perfect peace,* whose mind is *stayed* on thee: *because he trusteth in thee"* (Isaiah 26:3).

If we *really do* trust in the Lord, then we'll *keep* our minds on Him, *not* on the problems in our lives. Our Father tells us that *this* is the way to experience *perfect peace*—a peace which is *so* perfect that *no* problems can ever disturb it.

61 Of Course We Will Have Problems, But Keep On Reading...

God's Word clearly tells us that Christians *will* have problems, but the Scriptures *don't* stop there. Keep on reading:

First Part Of Scripture:

We Will Have Problems

"Many are the afflictions of the righteous...

"...in the world ye *shall* have tribulation...

Second Part Of Scripture:

We Can Overcome Them Through The Lord

"but the Lord delivereth him out of them *all"* (Psalm 34:15).

"but be of *good cheer;* I have *overcome* the world" (John 16:33).

62 We Should Actually Welcome Problems

When problems come into our lives, we should actually *welcome* them. Many Christians fail to realize that *our problems* are actually *God's opportunities.* God goes into action *where we leave off.* Therefore, He needs to have problems that we can't handle. He'll take care of these problems to the exact degree that we, (a) *let go* of them and, (b) *trust* Him to solve them.

The *best* thing that every happened to me in my entire life was coming face to face with financial ruin and a nervous breakdown in 1974. Because I got myself in such a mess, I *realized* that I was way over my head and I *willingly* studied and meditated day and night in God's Word. "It is *good* for me that I have been *afflicted;* that I might *learn* thy statutes. The law of thy mouth is *better* unto me than thousands of gold and silver" (Psalm 119:71-72).

It sounds very strange to most people when I say that we should be happy when we encounter trials and tribulations in our lives. However, God's Word definitely tells us that this *is* how we should react. As a result, our faith will be *proven* by these trials. Our faith will be *strengthened*, we will become more patient and dealing with these trials will cause

us to become *perfected* in our spiritual
development:

"Consider it wholly joyful, my brethren,
whenever you are enveloped in or encounter
trials of any sort, or fall into various *temptations.* Be assured and understand that the trial
and *proving of your faith* bring out *endurance*
and *steadfastness* and *patience.* But let endurance and steadfastness and patience have *full
play* and do a *thorough work,* so that you may
be (people) *perfectly and fully developed* (with
no defects), *lacking in nothing"* (James 1:2-4
The Amplified Bible).

Problems in our lives are actually *opportunities* to develop a stronger faith, greater
endurance and greater patience—qualities that
would *not* have developed to this degree *if*
these particular problems hadn't come into our
lives.

63 Faith And Patience Go Together

Faithful *and* patient Christians inherit the
promises of God. "...be not slothful, but followers of them who through *faith* and *patience*
inherit the promises" (Hebrews 5:12). *When* do
we actually obtain God's promises? "...*after* he
had *patiently endured,* he obtained the promise" (Hebrews 6:15).

God's promises tell us what He will do, but *not* when He will do it. We must leave the timing *up to Him.* "To *everything* there is a season, and a time to every purpose under the heaven..." (Ecclesiastes 3:1).

Many people give up too soon. Our Father is faithful. He *will* answer *if* we'll just believe and keep on believing patiently until He is *ready* to respond to our faith and our patience. "And let us *not* lose heart and grow weary and faint in acting nobly and doing right, for *in due time and at the appointed season* we *shall* reap, *if* we do not loosen and relax our courage and faint" (Galatians 6:9 *The Amplified Bible).*

64 Give The Seed A Chance To Grow

Patience is required in order to let God's Word produce its result. It needs to be *planted,* it needs to *take root,* then a *leaf* starts to form, then it grows *larger* and *finally* it is *ripe* and ready to be *harvested.* "...the *seed* should spring and *grow up,* he knoweth not how. For the earth bringeth forth fruit of herself; *first* the *blade, then* the *ear, after that* the *full corn* in the ear. But when the fruit is *brought forth,* immediately he putteth in the sickle because the *harvest is come"* (Mark 4:27-29).

Too many of us are *losing* the harvest

because we're expecting to receive it *before* the seed has a chance to grow. We need to realize that God has His time for everything and if we'll keep planting those seeds and keep waiting patiently, everything will work out just fine.

65 When We Overcome Problems, This Proves That Christianity Does Work

How can we ever expect our friends and loved ones to get excited about Christianity *if* they see us getting discouraged? *Why* should they want what we have? They *already know* how to get discouraged!

Do your words and your actions in the midst of tribulation clearly show your unwavering faith in God's Word and God's Holy Spirit living inside of you? *Have you* paid the price of building a faith that is unshakeable and unwavering, no matter what happens to you?

When the bottom is falling out, *this* is when Christians should *shine. This* is when our friends and loved ones should see *how well* Christian principles of faith *really do* work. *This* is when many people should look at us and decide that they *want* what we have!

66 Believers Should Be Able To Relax Under Pressure

The Bible contains over three thousand promises from our Father. If we *know* and *believe* a large number of these promises, *why* should we *ever* get upset about *anything??* If we *really do* believe, instead of struggling and straining and worrying, we will *relax* because we *know* that our Father *will* do *exactly* what His Word says He'll do—*if* we don't block Him through unbelief.

Many of us might *think* that we believe, but *if* we become tense, agitated and worked up when tribulations come upon us, we clearly show that we really *don't* trust the Lord. *No matter what* problems we might be faced with, Jesus Christ has won a *victory* over this particular problem. "...in *all* these things we are *more* than conquerors *through him* that loved us" (Romans 8:37).

Jesus won a total and complete victory. "...*All* power is given unto me in heaven and in earth" (Matthew 28:18). His victory is *our* victory. "Behold, *I give unto you power* to tread on serpents and scorpions, and *over all the power of the enemy:* and *nothing shall by any means hurt you*" (Luke 10:19). If we *really do* believe these words, then we'll *always* remain relaxed, *no matter* how difficult the problems might seem to be.

67 We Need To Be Still— God Is In Charge

Imagine a group of people trying to learn to swim. In a group like this, some of the would-be swimmers always thrash and splash when they're "on their own" in the water. Why do they do this? They do this because they won't "let go" and *trust* the water to *hold them up.*

Good swimmers *trust* the water. They *relax* in the water and they glide along almost *effortlessly. This* is how God wants us to live our lives. Instead of thrashing and splashing and trying to do everything by ourselves, we need to *let go* and *trust* the Lord to hold us up.

Our Father *won't* let us fall. He *is* there waiting to catch us in His arms if we'll just trust Him. "The eternal God *is* thy refuge, and underneath *are* the everlasting arms..." (Deuteronomy 33:27). When we come upon hard times, our Father wants us to do our best and then to calm down because we *know* that He is in charge. *"Be still* and *know* that I am God..."* (Psalm 46:10).

68 We Shouldn't Try To Figure Everything Out

Too many Christians struggle trying to figure everything out with intellectual reasoning. We can find answers to problems in the *natural* realm with our minds, but the prob-

59

lems of the *spiritual* realm require an entirely *different* solution. "Trust in the *Lord* with *all thine heart;* and *lean not unto thine own understanding.* In *all* thy ways *acknowledge him,* and *he* shall direct thy paths" (Proverbs 3:5-6).

God's Word clearly tells us that we *shouldn't* depend upon our human understanding. We *don't* have the answers to the difficult problems of life. Our understanding is too *limited.* "...the way of man is *not* in himself: it is *not* in man that walketh to direct his steps" (Jeremiah 10:23). "Man's goings are *of the Lord; how* can a man then understand his own way?" (Proverbs 20:24).

In the spiritual realm, our human intellectual understanding comes up empty. It just *doesn't* have the answers. These verses of Scripture clearly tell us that *only the Lord* has the answers. When the going is tough in any area of our lives, we have to be able to *let go* and put our trust *completely* in Him with *all* of our hearts, acknowledging in all our ways that He *does* direct our paths.

69 Do You Know Exactly How Your Faith Is Measured?

Sooner or later, severe tests come into all of our lives. When these crisis times come, our Father wants us to be ready. We should have prepared for these tests through several years of filling our minds and hearts with His Word.

I believe that many Christians *think* that they have more faith than they really do. There is a method by which we can measure *exactly* how strong our faith is. Do you know how our faith is measured in the spiritual realm? Do you know *exactly* how we show how deeply we believe?

Our faith is measured specifically and exactly by, (a) what we *say* and, (b) by what we *do* when we are under severe pressure. When the going is tough, our words and actions show *exactly* how strong our faith is.

Many of us *start out* strong, but how strong does that faith *remain* as the pressure keeps coming against it? *Do* our words and actions stay the same? Or, *do* they become more hesitant and doubting as the hours and days (and perhaps weeks and months) go by???

Look back at the most recent crisis times in your life. *How well* have you scored on these tests of faith? Whether it was an automobile breakdown, family problem, health problem, financial problem or any other kind of problem, *did you* get worked up and upset? Or, *did you* stay calm, constantly *speaking God's Word and doing* exactly what God's Word says to do?

20 In Times Of Pressure, Our Words Must Continually Acknowledge The Total Victory of Jesus Christ

Christians should never allow words of failure or defeat to come out of their mouths. When and if we allow this to happen, these words clearly *deny* the total and complete victory that Jesus Christ has won for us. Philippians 4:13 says that we *can* do *all* things through the strength of Jesus Christ. If we allow our mouths to say otherwise, this places limits on "The Limitless One."

God's Word says, "If any man speak, let him speak as *the oracles of God...*" (I Peter 4:11). The Greek word that is translated *oracles* means *God's spoken word."* This means that the words that we speak with our mouths should *line up with* what God's Word says.

This is especially important when the bottom falls completely out—if the doctor says that it's cancer, if someone whom we love is tragically killed or if the bottom falls out emotionally, financially or in any other area. *This* is when the words that we say are carefully measured and when the results that we receive are based on these words.

21 How Can We Control The Words That We Speak During Moments Of Crisis?

When the pressure is really tough, *how* can we control the words that come out of our mouths? One thing is certain—we can't bring our words under control with human *will power*. "...the human tongue can be tamed by *no* man..." (James 3:8 *The Amplified Bible*). When the pressure is immense, will power is *never* sufficient. As much as we might want to control our tongues, we *cannot* control them continually through the power of our will. Sooner or later, we'll weaken if this is our only hope.

Jesus told us exactly what controls the words that we speak. "...*out of the abundance of the heart* the mouth speaketh. A *good* man out of the good treasure of the heart bringeth forth *good* things: and an *evil* man out of the evil treasure bringeth forth *evil* things" (Matthew 12:34-35).

When the pressure is immense, the words that come out of our mouths will *show* what we *believe* deep down in our *hearts*. We need to diligently fill our hearts with God's Word so that our hearts will be filled *abundantly* when moments of crisis come into our lives.

22 The Name Of Jesus Has Immense Spiritual Power

I meditate on the Word of God and I speak the Word of God over and over every day of my life. I want very much to "program my computer" so that it will be properly programmed for the crises of life.

I also speak the Name of Jesus Christ constantly. This Name has immense spiritual power. "Wherefore God also hath highly exalted him, and given him a name which is *above* every name; *that at the name of Jesus every knee should bow, of things in heaven, and things in earth, and things under the earth...*" (Philippians 2:9-10).

The Name of Jesus is *so* powerful in the spiritual realm that *every* knee must bow before it—here on this earth, in heaven and beneath this earth. Our Father *commands* us to believe in the power of this Name. "And this is his *commandment*, That we should *believe on the name of his Son Jesus Christ...*" (I John 3:23). No matter where we are, we should *always* call upon that Name. "...in *every* place call upon the name of Jesus Christ our Lord..." (I Corinthians 1:2).

Whatever we say and *whatever* we do should be done in the Name of Jesus Christ. "And *whatsoever* ye do in word or deed do *all* in the name of the Lord Jesus..." (Colossians 3:17). When we use this Name with faith, this brings *blessings* into our lives. "...*Blessed* is he that cometh in the name of the Lord" (Luke 13:35).

We should speak the name of Jesus over and over every day of our lives. Often I just say "Jesus"... "Jesus"... "Jesus" again and again and again. I say it softly with love. Sometimes I sing it. Other times I say it boldly with authority. There is *immense* spiritual power in this Name.

23 Our Prayers Must Agree With God's Will

Many times we don't receive answers to our prayers because we're *not* praying according to our Father's will for our lives. Although we may not understand, many of the prayers that God hears from His children each day would actually *hurt us* if He answered them. What Father would intentionally hurt his children? Our heavenly Father doesn't want to hurt us either.

So, His Word tells us *not* to pray for selfish desires. "Ye ask, and *receive not*, because ye ask amiss, that ye may consume it upon your *lusts*" (James 4:3). We need to pray according to our Father's *will*. How can we be *sure* that we pray according to His will?

We can be sure to the exact degree that we have paid the price of continual study and meditation in His Word. The more we do this, the more our thoughts, desires and plans will *line up* with His will for our lives. Then, we can pray according to His will, *knowing* that He *hears us* and *knowing* that He *will* answer:

"And this is the *confidence* that we have in him, that, *if we ask any thing according to his will, he heareth us:* and if we *know* that he *hear us, whatsoever* we ask, *we know that we have the petitions that we desired of him*" (I John 5:14-15).

24 Prayers Shouldn't Be "Begging," "Pleading" Prayers

"We *shouldn't* go to our Father with "begging," "pleading" prayers. *Instead,* we should find *promises* in God's Word that answer our prayers. When we go to our Father in prayer, we should pray *in faith* based upon these *promises* in His Word. *This* is how we need to pray if we expect to receive from God. "...I will pray unto the Lord your God *according to your words,* and it *shall* come to pass..." (Jeremiah 42:4).

25 Instead Of Criticizing Government Leaders, We Should Pray For Them

Instead of *criticizing* governmental leaders, we should *pray* for them. Criticism *tears them down*. God's Word tells us to release our faith to ask God to *bless* those leaders and *lift them up*. "By the *blessing* of the upright the city is *exalted:* but it is *overthrown* by the mouth of the wicked" (Proverbs 11:11).

All of us want to live in a world of peace. God's Word tells us the way to do this is to pray regularly for those who are in positions of authority and responsibility. "Here are my directions: pray *much* for others; plead for God's *mercy* upon them; *give thanks* for all He is going to do for them. Pray in this way for kings and all others who are in *authority* over us, or are in places of *high responsibility,* so that we can *live in peace and quietness,* spending our time in godly living and thinking much about the Lord" (I Timothy 2:1-2 *The Living Bible).*

Are you praying regularly for local, state and national leaders??

26 We Need To Do What God's Word Tells Us To Do

In the spiritual realm, our words are very, very important and so are our actions. Our Father has given us a Book to tell us exactly how He wants us to live our lives. It is our duty to study this Book constantly to see what our Father wants us to do and then to *do* what His Book tells us to do.

It is a sin to ignore the instructions of our Father. God's Word is speaking to us. *How* can any Christian justify ignoring our Father's instructions to us? *This* is how we receive blessings from our Father. "...if *anyone keeps looking steadily* into God's laws for free men he will not only *remember* it but he will *do what it says,* and God *will greatly bless him in everything he does."* (James 1:25 *The Living Bible*).

When crisis times come in your life will your heart and mind be so full of God's Word that you will boldly *speak* that Word in moments of crisis and automatically *do* what it says to do no matter how difficult the problems might be?

22 Faith Without Works Is Dead

On three different occasions in the second chapter of James (verses 17, 20 and 26) we are told that "faith without works is *dead.*" The Greek word that is translated *works* means *action.* If we don't take *action* based upon our faith, this faith is *lifeless.* It is like a *corpse.* It has *no* spiritual value. We bring our faith to life only to the degree that we *act* on it.

One time Jesus' mother, Mary, and His brothers couldn't get to Him because of the great crowds that surrounded Him. When He was told that they were waiting to see Him, He said, "...My mother and my brethren are these which *hear* the word of God, and *do* it" (Luke 8:21). *Do you* qualify as a brother (or sister) of Jesus Christ by this definition??

If we want our Father to bless us, we need to learn everything that we can from His Word and then *do* what His Word tells us to do. "...*blessed* are they that *hear* the word of God, and *keep* it" (Luke 11:28).

Our Father wants us to fill our hearts and our mouths with His Word for one reason. "...the word is *very nigh* unto thee, in thy mouth, and in thy *heart*, that thou mayest *do* it" (Deuteronomy 30:14). We *must* step out in faith on the Word of God. If we're *afraid* to do this, we're showing clearly in the spiritual realm that we really don't believe that our Father will do what his Word says that He will do.

28 Our Words And Actions Must Show Persistent, Unwavering Faith

In the natural realm, if we want the muscles in our bodies to grow stronger, we use them against opposing forces. This is why people exercise and lift weights. Spiritual development is similar to muscular development. We need to *use* our faith against strong opposing forces. *This* is how faith grows.

God's Word tells us to "Fight the *good fight* of faith..." (I Timothy 6:12). If we are able to fight a *good* fight of faith, then we also must be able to fight a *bad* fight of faith. A bad fight of faith *does not persist.* When the going gets tough, it *wavers,* and *backs* off.

Our Father wants us to develop our faith to the point where it is *solid, unwavering* and *unshakeable,* just like the mountain of Zion where He lives. "They that trust in the Lord shall be as mount Zion, which *cannot be removed,* but abideth forever" (Psalm 125:1). Our faith in God's Word should be so strong that we are always *single-minded.* We should be so single-minded that we *never* give in to what we hear or what we see or how we feel.

Double-minded Christians go back and forth between what they see, what they hear, how they feel and what God's Word says. This double-mindedness *stops* us from receiving from God. "...ask in faith, *nothing wavering.* For he that wavereth is like a wave of the sea driven with the wind and tossed. For *let not that man think that he shall receive any thing of the Lord.* A double-minded man is *unstable* in *all* his ways" (James 1:6-8).

Conclusion

God's laws work whether we know about them or not. Ignorance of a law doesn't affect its working. All around us the laws of physics, chemistry, electricity, etc. are working constantly whether or not we understand how they work.

Since God's laws work every day in each of our lives, it makes sense to learn *all* that we can about how they work. In this book, I have given you 78 scriptural "nuggets" on the subject of faith. These nuggets explain great truths from God's Word in a simple and concise manner.

Difficult times are coming in this world. In the midst of all of the afflictions that will be coming, the world will see a group of people who have risen above these difficult times and are coping beautifully with them. This group of people will consist of those Christians who have paid the price of studying God's Word, believing it and acting on it. I pray that you will be a member of this unique group of Christians.

Appendix

Have You Entered

Into The Kingdom Of God?

You have just read an explanation of several verses of scripture on the subject of faith. God's laws of faith are laws that our Father has written for His children—those human beings who have entered into His kingdom. I ask each reader of this book, "Have *you* entered into the kingdom of God?"

Jesus Christ said, "...Verily, verily, I say unto thee, except a man be *born again,*he *cannot* see the kingdom of God" (John 3:3). Jesus went on to say, "...ye *must* be born again" (John 3:7). It is very clear that there is only one way to enter into the kingdom of God and that is to "be born again."

We don't enter into God's kingdom by church attendance, by teaching Sunday school, by baptism, by confirmation or by living a good life. Jesus Christ paid the price for every one of us to enter into God's kingdom, but this is not "automatic." Many people are so caught up with their own religious denomination or their own personal beliefs that they completely miss God's specific instructions as to how to enter into His kingdom—for the rest of our lives on earth and also for eternity in heaven.

In order to become a born-again Christian, we first of all must admit that we are sinners (Romans 3:23, James 2:10). We must admit that there is absolutely no way that we can enter into God's kingdom based upon our own merits. Next, we have to genuinely repent of our sins (Luke 13:3, Acts 3:19).

After this admission of sin and repentance there is one additional step that must be taken in order to become a born-again Christian. "For if you *tell others* with your own mouth that Jesus Christ is your Lord, and *believe* in your own heart that God has raised Him from the dead, you *will* be saved. For it is by believing in his *heart* that a man becomes right with God; and with his *mouth* he tells others of his faith, confirming his salvation" (Romans 10:9-10 *The Living Bible*).

Many people know that Jesus Christ died for our sins. However, knowledge isn't enough. Intellectual agreement isn't enough. In order to be born again, we have to accept Jesus as our Saviour in our *hearts* and not just in our heads. We're not born again until we come to Him as admitted sinners and trust Him deep down in our hearts as the only way that we can enter into the kingdom of God. God knows exactly what we believe deep down in our hearts (I Samuel 16:7, I Chronicles 28:9, Hebrews 4:13).

We must believe in our hearts that Jesus Christ is the Son of God, that He was born of a virgin, that He died on the cross to pay for our sins, that He rose again from the dead and that he lives today. In order to be a born-again Christian, Romans 10:9-10 tells us that we must not only believe this in our hearts, but we *also* must open our *mouths* and tell others of this belief. This confirms our salvation.

When you believe this in your heart and tell others of this belief with your mouth, *then* you are a born-again Christian. All of us were born naturally on the day that our mothers gave birth to us. We must have a second birth—a spiritual birth—in order to enter into God's kingdom. "For you have a new life. It was not passed on to you from your parents, for the life they gave you will fade away. This new one will last forever, for it comes from Christ, God's ever-living Message to men" (I Peter 1:23 *The Living Bible).*

God wants us to come to Him, not as intellectuals, but as little children. God doesn't reveal Himself to us through our intellects. He reveals Himself to us through our hearts and, in order to enter into His kingdom, we must come to Him as little children. We may be adults in the natural world, but in the spiritual world we have to start all over. We have to be born again as spiritual babies. Jesus said, "...except ye be converted and become as little children, ye shall not enter into the kingdom of heaven" (Matthew 18:3).

The following prayer will cause you to become born again if you believe this in your heart and open your mouth and tell others of this belief:

"Dear Father, I come to you in the Name of Jesus Christ. I admit that I am a sinner and I know that there is no way that I can enter into your kingdom based upon the sinful life that I have led. I'm genuinely sorry for my sins and I ask for your mercy. I believe in my heart that Jesus Christ is your Son—that He was born of a virgin, that He died on the cross to pay for my sins, that you raised Him from the dead and that He is alive today. I trust in Him as my only way of entering into your kingdom. I confess now to you, Father, that Jesus Christ is my Saviour and my Lord and I will tell others of this decision now and in the future. Thank you, Father. Amen."

When you believe this in your heart and confess this to others with your mouth, you have been reborn spiritually. You are brand new in the spiritual realm. "Therefore if any man be in Christ, he is a *new* creature: old things are *passed away;* behold, *all* things become new" (II Corinthians 5:17).

Now that you have a new, recreated spirit, you are ready to study, understand and obey God's laws of prosperity and all of His other laws. This will transform the rest of your life on earth and you also will live forever in heaven. "For God so loved the world, that he gave his only begotten son, that whosoever believeth in him should not perish, but have everlasting life" (John 3:16).

A Request To Our Readers

Has this book helped you? If so, would you be willing to tell others so that this book can help them too? Many people are naturally skeptical about the advertising claims for a book such as this. This is why we use a large number of "testimonials" from satisfied readers in our advertising for this book.

If this book has helped you, I'd appreciate it if you would write to me in care of the publisher. Please tell me in your own words how this book has helped you and why you would recommend it to others. Please give us as much information as you can.

Also, we will need your written permission to use any part or all of your comments, your name and the town or city that you live in (we never use street addresses) for our advertising for this book.

Thank you for helping us and, most important, for helping others.

Jack Hartman
Word Associates
P.O. Box 3293
Manchester, NH 03105

Another Book By . . .
Jack Hartman

Jack Hartman is a self-employed businessman. In 1974, he was on the verge of bankruptcy and a nervous breakdown. He was almost paralyzed by worry and fear. At that time he accepted Jesus Christ as Saviour and Lord.

He immediately started to study and meditate day and night in the Holy Scriptures to learn how to solve his financial and emotional problems. After several months of study he was able to apply these Biblical principles to his problems and they worked!

His business has turned completely around, all debts have been paid off right on schedule and his business has grown steadily each year since then. In addition, he and three other businessmen started a Bible study class in his office which now has grown into a large church with average Sunday morning attendance between 900 and 1,000 people.

The growth of this business and the growth of this church have come as a result of applying Biblical principles which Jack has explained in his book *Trust God For Your Finances*.

The principles in this book are not theoretical. They have worked in Jack Hartman's life and in the lives of many people who have counseled with him. Now these principles are available in book form.

Jack carefully points out the differences between the world's system of prosperity and God's laws of prosperity. He explains that all of the warnings in the Bible against financial prosperity are warnings against following the *world's* system of prosperity.

Our Father very *definitely* wants His children to prosper as long as they follow His laws of prosperity. These laws are laid out in detail in sixteen chapters of specific instruction—every chapter filled with many verses of scripture.

Trust God For Your Finances can be ordered for $4.95 per copy plus 10% postage and handling. The order form for this is at the end of this book.

Cassette Tapes
By Jack Hartman

Tape #	Title
01H	**How To Study The Bible (Part I)**—21 scriptural reasons why it is so important to study the Bible.
02H	**How To Study The Bible (Part II)**—a step-by-step detailed explanation of a proven effective system for studying the Bible (our most demanded tape).
03H	**Enter Into God's Rest**—Don't struggle and strain with loads that are too heavy for you. Learn exactly what God's Word teaches about relaxing under pressure.
04H	**Freedom From Worry—**a comprehensive scriptural explanation on how to become completely free from worry.
05H	**God's Strength—Our Weakness**—God's strength is available to the degree that we can admit our human weakness and trust, instead, in His unlimited strength.
06H	**How To Transform Our Lives**—a thorough scriptural study of how we can change our lives completely through a complete spiritual renewal of our minds.
07H	**The Greatest Power In The Universe (Part I)**—The greatest power in the universe is love. Part I gives a beautiful scriptural explanation of our Father's love for us.
08H	**The Greatest Power In The Universe (Part II)**—a thorough scriptural explanation on our love for God, our love for each other and overcoming fear through love.
09H	**How Well Do You Know Jesus Christ?**—an Easter Sunday message that received great audience response. After this message, you'll know Jesus Christ as you never knew Him before.
10H	**God's Perfect Peace**—In a world of unrest, people everywhere are searching for inner peace. This is a detailed scriptural explanation of how to obtain God's perfect peace.
11H	**Freedom Through Surrender**—Millions of people are trying to find freedom by "doing their own thing." God's Word tells us to do just the opposite. Freedom comes only as a result of daily surrender of our lives to Jesus Christ.

Book and Cassette Tape Order Form

To order books and cassette tapes by Jack Hartman, please use this order form:

Book Or Cassette Tape	# of Copies	Total Price
Trust God For Your Finances ($4.95 ea.)	_____	$_____
Nuggets Of Faith ($2.50 ea.)	_____	$_____
Cassette tapes ($4.00 ea. - $3.00 ea. if three or more tapes are ordered).		

Check the tapes that you wish to order.

___ 01H	___ 02H	___ 03H	___ 04H
___ 05H	___ 06H	___ 07H	___ 08H
___ 09H	___ 10H	___ 11H	_____ $_____

Total Price — Books and Tapes	$_____
Add 10% Postage and Handling	_____
Enclosed Check or Money Order	$_____

Make check payable to: Word Associates
Mail order to: P.O. Box 3293
Manchester, NH 03105

Please print your name and address **clearly**:

Name _____

Address _____

City _____

State or Province _____

Zip or Postal Code _____

Foreign orders must be submitted in U␣
Foreign orders are shipped by unin␣
all orders within 48 hours of rec␣
We will give you a full refu␣
you are dissatisfied in an␣